Winter Woman

Winter Woman

Poems by

Jennifer Lynn Soule

© 2024 Jennifer Lynn Soule. All rights reserved.
This material may not be reproduced in any form, published,
reprinted, recorded, performed, broadcast,
rewritten, or redistributed without
the explicit permission of Jennifer Lynn Soule.
All such actions are strictly prohibited by law.

Cover photo by Unsplash (Lena Polishko)
Author photo by Michelle Powell

ISBN: 978-1-63980-606-5

Kelsay Books
502 South 1040 East, A-119
American Fork, Utah 84003
Kelsaybooks.com

To all the peoples and landscapes of South Dakota—
Indigenous and settlers—including my dear mother,
Leone Egger Kayl, and my late husband, Brad Soule,
who loved South Dakota as his adopted home state.

Acknowledgments

So many people have helped me bring this book to fruition that I could never name all my friends and poetry partners who over the years have read these poems at various stages. I do want to thank Lee Ann Roripaugh, my MFA mentor at University of Nebraska, who was a tremendous help with the final structure of this book.

My gratitude goes to my friend/writing partner, Linda Tate, who has probably read more versions of these poems than anyone, and who has offered guidance and support for my work throughout the years. Also, I deeply appreciate all the time and help from many friends and other writing partners along the way. This includes my late husband, who was always my first and last reader.

Of course, many thanks go to Karen Kelsay and the staff at Kelsay Books for bringing this collection of poems into the world to share with others. I am most grateful.

Thanks also go to Finishing Line Press for publishing my chapbook, *Hiawatha Asylum,* in which some of the poems in this collection appeared. Additionally, my appreciation goes out to Cherry Grove Collections for publishing my poetry collection *Postcard Days.*

I also wish to acknowledge and thank the journals and small presses that have published my previous work:

Journals:
Briar Cliff Review: "Feral Peacocks"
Coal City Review: "Bald Eagles"
Coal Hill Review: "Finding Hiawatha"
Hurricane Review: "Fourth-Grade Flashback"
Modern Haiku: "A Time for Herons"

Plainsongs: "Goodwill"
South Dakota Journal of Medicine: "Snow Geese"
South Dakota Magazine: "Homeless at McDonald's"
South Dakota Review: "Hiawatha Asylum for Insane Indians," "Morning Takes"
The Sow's Ear Poetry Review: "Directions to the Vineyard," "Smoking Mr. V"
Vermillion Literary Project: "December on the Great Plains"

Anthologies:
I Walked by the River, Brandyn Johnson, editor. (Sioux Falls, SD: Scurfpea Publishing, 2016): "New in Town," "Weddings," "Winter Woman"
Memory Echo Words, Norma C. Wilson, editor. (Sioux Falls, SD: Scurfpea Publishing, 2014): "Anomie" and "Sheriff's Log"

Contents

I   Great Plains Roots: Home of Wind and Sky

Directions to the Vineyard	17
September Departs, Sioux Falls, 2001	18
December on the Great Plains	20
Raccoon Moon	21
Border Town	22
Wind	23
Snow Geese	24
November Sunset	25
South Dakota Summer Vacation (circa 1957)	26
Weddings	27
Sister Express	28
Sheriff's Log: Custer County, South Dakota*	29
New in Town	31
Butterflies and Grandmothers	32
Jams	33
Winter Woman	34
Morning Takes	35
Fourth-Grade Flashback	36
Moon Ride	38
A Time for Herons	39
Stargazing at Noon	40
Wounded Knee Horseback Ride (December 28, 2000)	41

II   Hiawatha Asylum

Finding Hiawatha	45
South Dakota Senator Richard Pettigrew's Senate Floor Plea, 1899	46

How to Get Committed to the Hiawatha Asylum for Insane Indians	47
Augustana Academy Student Writes Her Family (September 8, 1929)	49
Dr. Silk Writes Home (March 20, 1929)	50
Long Time Owl Woman Haunts the Canton Hospital	51
Dr. Silk Writes Home (March 21, 1929)	52
Yells At Night	53
Dr. Silk Writes Home (March 22, 1929)	54
Augustana Academy Student Writes Family (October 4, 1929)	55
Dr. Silk Writes Home (March 23, 1929)	56
Hiawatha Volunteer	57
Dr. Silk Writes Home (March 24, 1929)	58
Dr. Hummer Defends Himself	60
Night Train	61
Death at Hiawatha	62
Dr. Silk Writes Home (March 25, 1929)	63
Canton Farmer Remembers	64
Long Time Owl Woman Haunts Hiawatha Golf Course	65

III   Branching Out: Looking for Home

The Inner Circle	69
Smoking Mr. V	71
Evening Shift	72
Hotel Hot Springs	73
Rock Man	74
Anomie	75

Surplus Beans	77
Bookstore Church	78
Goodwill	79
Hannah's House:	
A Shelter for Women and Children	80
Seeing Myself	89
Blackberry Winter: A Southern Term	90
A Few Wars Ago: Levertov's "At the	
Justice Department November 15, 1969"	91
Snapshots in Haiku	92
Upper Peninsula of Michigan	94
Feral Peacocks	95
Benita's Photo	96
Homeless at McDonald's	97

*Extreme. Perhaps the key word for Dakota . . .
What happens with extremes is that they come together,
and the result is a kind of tension.*
—John R. Milton, *South Dakota: A History*

I

Great Plains Roots: Home of Wind and Sky

*Now there's only a red-tailed
hawk, hanging on the wind, hunting;
a poet passing by.*
—Linda Hasselstrom, "Driving to Red Scaffold,"
Land Circle: Writings Collected from the Land

Directions to the Vineyard

Turn left beside the red-tailed hawk
on the third bale of hay. Note a peacock
farm screaming turquoise through the fence.
Dry in late June heat, follow Dolphin Road—
dust black earth along a river trickle
where cows stare. Left again at two dappled
horses swishing flies with tails once used
for making chairs, when land held wishes
before stars were bought and sold. Listen
for the strains of a fiddle breakdown ghosting
over the hill with the smell of bacon. Follow
sparrows to the ravine where lush vines
tangle on fences, grapes ripen red
as ribbons carried in by foxes
who know about following the hawk home.

September Departs, Sioux Falls, 2001

"Man's Head Explodes in Barber's Chair."
That strange headline stuck now,
like an awful ad jingle, although I can't recall
my grandmother's middle name
or any lines from *Beowulf.*

Thirty days a difference makes
as news fills with terrorism:
funerals, jihad, Red Cross,
firemen, New York, bagpipes.
No solace in autumn equinox.

We transplant geraniums, begonias,
several iris tubers—a neighbor's gift.
Reports of poverty's decline
unnoticed, unemployment soars.
Quiet reigns in shaded rubble.

Fewer contrails scrawl the South Dakota skies.

We set a circle of chrysanthemums.
High schools hold parades,
homecomings. Flags everywhere—
flown, worn, taped in windows. The terrorists
opened shirts and cried to Allah at their end.

A sugar maple on our land
flies gold and red;
our jeans and T-shirts dry.
September darkened.

At Joe Foss airport
among bars and pizza stands,
the National Guard bears arms.
Red sumac burn along a country road.

September started cooler,
ended warmer, different
than when the month arrived
a safer world than now—

Moon When Leaves Turn Brown.

December on the Great Plains

Jazz, deceptively
soft in a warm house, outside
northwest wind travels cold
at forty miles an hour—
gusting more it captures snow
drives it like a herd of buffalo
over the Great Plains toward
Lake Superior or maybe
the Atlantic Ocean.
Humans stranded, left
like fools in tin boxes
wheels spinning.

Raccoon Moon

Washing the night blue,
it exposes more space than is possibly there,
spotlights a barren Dakota landscape.

Hungry animals use the light to hunt.
Coyotes slouch softly over the hill
while something small and furry runs ahead.

A crystal in a southern window
reflects moonlight
like chilled white wine—

not the prancing prism of daytime sun.

The air tonight is windless, clear, and dry,
warmer than recent weeks—a good night
to be out hunting or howling.

Border Town

Not long ago a young Lakota man
was found stuffed dead into a trash can.
A reconciliation group
meets to bring people together.

Mobridge, South Dakota on the Missouri,
straddles two countries—Indian
and White—cut off from the rest of the world
and each other by the river.

On the west side—Standing Rock Reservation,
Sitting Bull's fenced-in grave,
a monument to Sakakawea where
wind and white horses move together.

On the east side—a deserted,
shutters-banging-in-the-wind parochial
school called Central Indian Bible College.
A Starlight Motel discounts million-dollar
views of a water sunset on the Great Plains.

Residents cross the bridge daily
for gambling at the tribal casino,
shopping, and the Burger King.
City Hall, once an old high school,
now houses Oscar Howe murals, created
during the Depression as he painted
his way across borders with tempera.

Wind

Motorcycling in South Dakota
we become one with the wind
on the prairie, queen of green
and gold and humans too.
Flying down roads, we are
cornstalks dancing to exhaustion,
like the woman in red shoes.
Grasses bow to wind's power.
So do we willingly submit
and on curves,
commit to another plain
for the ride's duration.

Snow Geese

At dusk a shadow line
moves in the northern sky.
Monochromatic November
brightens, fills with snow geese.

Wings tipped black on luminous white,
they soar above snow-dusted fallow fields
honking their way down the valley
in graceful floppy heart-stopping *V*s.

Southbound toward the Gulf of Mexico,
at sixty miles an hour with the wind
they follow the Big Sioux River
to feeding stops on yet unfrozen water.

The summer breeding marshes
will wait their return in springtime,
cycles of birth and death,
from Gulf to tundra waste and back again.

The line of geese is fading in the south.
A landscape, in black and white, lies harvested,
barren, as Arctic air roars in tonight
claiming the Great Plains for an ancient grief.

November Sunset

I live at the edge of the Great Plains prairie. Sun sets early behind razorback ridges of the southern Black Hills. Home from work, I walk out to meet the sunset.

A summer sunset is a glass of wine, but the autumn sunset is only a sip in South Dakota. Thin lines of color wind around and among the clouds like a feather boa—the pinks, blues, violets, and reds mix with gray. Give texture and depth to the sky's canvas.

Even if only a sliver of a moment, to watch earth and sky end the day together sets my circadian clock. I'm a sunset woman. When the veil between worlds is thinner, I breathe more deeply, pause and delight. Walk west into day's end. Then return home before the mountain lions come out.

November sun
dropping day into soft pastels—
a mule deer hops home

South Dakota Summer Vacation (circa 1957)

The Plymouth is a covered wagon hitched
to the lamppost all night. Packed with pillows,
Tinkertoys, *Little House on the Prairie*,
a playpen, crayons, a smiling turtle,
and a Hula Hoop, it dreads the August trip
from Sioux Falls to Winner. Vacation means
a visit to Dad's relatives on the edge
of the Rosebud Indian Reservation
where ghosts and white horses graze
the shadows of the past. With crustless
bologna-Velveeta-cheese sandwiches
on Wonder Bread, we leave at dawn—
for this family, about 11:00 a.m. No, make that
noon. Outside of Lone Tree, the radiator
hisses and overheats. My Dad, not knowing
a carburetor from *a hill of beans,* gets out,
swears at the wind. Mom rattles the last drop
of coffee from the glass thermos. Nancy cries
to ride the horses. Jeff has already tripped
over a rock and sprained his big toe when
a medicine man in a pickup truck stops
and performs some magic with a wrench
to fix the car. We roll up to Aunt Goldie's
where she's waving her Camel and Schlitz,
glad we finally made it. The sun reddens
and purples down around the lone station wagon.

Weddings

An April Sunday brunch
at Casa Marina in Key West—
omelet, cheese blintz, prime rib, pear torte.
Cool breeze, sunny skies,
turquoise water lapping sand,
music live with Latin beat.
Further out, shrimp boats harvest the sea—
working overtime.

A lace-covered arch, a flurry of flowers,
a young woman in white
walks down a pebble path strewn with roses.
Fairy-tale wedding setting
with Caribbean rhythm—
sea and sky in mating dance.

Older voices: married, divorced, remarried
mix with the wedding march. Waitress Belinda
chimes in Australian accent, "Ah, two more lambs
to the slaughter." At scattered tables customers
murmur: "Hope they make it." "Arch to nowhere."

In another April, my parents
leave a small South Dakota church
in a snowstorm for their
Omaha honeymoon. Their wedding album
reveals a post-war couple, smiling.
A young woman in her new blue suit
and a young vet in topcoat wave goodbye.
Later they raised six children—
working overtime.

Sister Express

It is a South Dakota summer afternoon in the 1950s. Hot. Boring. I gather up my brother and sister for a red Ryder wagon adventure. As the eldest, I plan outings for the day. We are free to roam. This is before kids appear on milk cartons. No fears cloud our day.

My mother packs peanut-butter-and-jelly sandwiches on Wonder Bread with the crusts cut off. This makes them special. Also chocolate chip cookies. We are set.

Summit Park is the destination. It has swings and a merry-go-round. In the winter it is an ice-skating rink. The day is ours.

summer visit
to the old neighborhood—
doors all locked

Sheriff's Log: Custer County, South Dakota*

suspicious person walking south
on Highway 385—hitchhiking
from Washington to Colorado

motor home stuck in tunnel
on Iron Mountain Road

purple Suzuki reported
driving fast and recklessly
towards Rapid City

mute transient reported walking
towards Wyoming

deputies assisted with traffic
while cattle were moved
across Highway 16

possibly-sick turkey reported
at Hazelrodt Cutoff—Game, Fish,
and Parks contacted

two loose donkeys
on Lechner Lane

man on North Pole Road reported
two llamas missing
one brown, the other black-and-white spotted

buffalo walked into a neighbor's yard
owner contacted

dog or coyote reported
dragging its back end
near Taco John's

4:58 p.m.: a llama
reported out near
Comanche Campground

black lab spotted in
Jewel Cave area with snoot
full of porcupine quills

report received of a skunk
walking back and forth in front
of guest rooms at Custer motel

woman called Poison Control
daughter had brushed her teeth
with Icy Hot

deputies assisted Forest Service
in locating
lost pinecone gatherer

lawn ornaments reported stolen
depicted two fawns: faded blue
extra patrol requested

visiting brown llama
reported at residence

*found poem

New in Town

At the Dakota Lumberyard
we wait while glass is cut, keys made.
It's as much fun as watching soybeans dry,
so I wander up the street to Laurie's Café

where thirteen farmers sit in DeKalb seed caps,
drinking coffee, smoking cigarettes.
Women fry up eggs and griddle sausage,
serve coffee on the run and laugh at jokes.

At Laurie's, nine o'clock is late—
these men already worked
half of most people's days
to earn this midmorning break.

They notice the stranger, quiet down,
white café mugs poised for observation.
Coffee-to-go, I smile, head back
to lumberyard and husband, wondering

what they might wonder about me.
Wondering, too: Will my ancestors' blood
stir me to root here? Will I someday walk
into Laurie's and be asked, *The usual?*

Butterflies and Grandmothers

The butterflies belonged
to grandmothers who grew the flowers
and understood the need

for color and movement
in a prairie garden on the plains
with its grand murals of earth and sky

changing constantly with seasons
and storms. Flowers and butterflies
tended close to home.

Grandmothers knew about
crafting a cradle from a bread basket
to keep a twin preemie warm

near the wood stove. Adaptability
a skill learned early, like making
rhubarb pie or delivering babies.

Belief in the ability to emerge
from a cocoon and kiss a red zinnia
or swing on a hollyhock

essential for survival. Akin
to the owl butterfly who spreads
its wings wide to mimic the face

of its namesake and scare small birds.
Such myths don't always protect.
But if spared, a few will fly

on ragged wings, learn to live
and love what remains. Make do.

Jams

Today my husband and I make plum jam—
it seems easier than making jelly
or preserves—just two ingredients.
Plums and seriously unhealthy amounts
of processed white sugar produces
sweet purple glow in six glass Mason jars.

My grandmother put up wild plums and blackberries
herself while my grandfather tended cows.
She finished before the sun heated up
the kitchen—unlike us working late into afternoon
exasperated with the hot slow thickening
of pulp. Stirring stirring stirring.

My grandmother tried college for awhile
but went home to farm and family.
I thought a PhD would help me avoid
all that intensive household drudgery.
My ancestors endured, and I left home.
But I've come full circle now
to harvesting and putting up.

Winter Woman

One must have a mind of winter
   —Wallace Stevens

It's snowing lightly on the Black Hills. A gentle snow like soft Irish rain. And it's cold. A good day to stay in with chicken soup and Gypsy Cold Cure tea as I feel a cold coming on. But a woman born of winter, I can enjoy the season and endure.

Endurance and survival were my first early-woman lessons. January: the coldest month. Anniversary of the Children's Blizzard. At only five pounds, I was swaddled and held close. Learned there are warm places in cold, harsh times.

As a woman who had to love winter, I needed to discover its secrets. To love the quiet, slowed-down time of the year. Season of solitude. A time necessary to nourish the Self. I was lucky to learn this early. Still, at times I forget. But when the snow falls, I'm nudged to light candles on the dark day, build a fire, and make hot chocolate with marshmallows. Time to remember those early lessons.

sunday snow
white on ponderosa pines—
quiet woman's day

Morning Takes

Groggy, morning wakes
under a prairie canopy. Crows
caw at false light—half-hearted
in cool March air, dense fog,
landscape a seascape.
Pheasants desperate for food
run in frozen cornfields.
We make love at first light.
Bodies sensing spring
wake early—eager, wilder
creatures needing to mate.
Morning geese fly overhead.
Coyote howls behind a hill.
Animals are on the prowl.

Fourth-Grade Flashback

Something about family continuity—
a string of stories, tattered photographs
surfacing unexpectedly like lost socks.

Thanksgiving, my nephew's wife
arrived with surprise photographs.
My fourth-grade teacher, Miss McGowan,

took them in 1957, kept them
ever since. Portraits in black and white
her Palmer penmanship listing us all.

The photos show a baby-boomer
crop of thirty-one. 124
arms and legs of mischief.

Here is Loren, who would be
my first boyfriend, standing
next to my friend Barbara and me.

She played the flute and wed a farmer.
A little boy now dead from AIDS.
These went off to Vietnam.

What became of David Weewee? Gordie
Eggebraaten? Rough names
for little boys. Little we all were,

girls "more mature" than
prepubescent boys!
Smarter too, sassy, playful.

I see those poodles on the skirts,
hear the rock and roll:
Danny and the Juniors' "At the Hop."

The local movie theater featured
Bridge on the River Kwai. My parents
talked of Sputnik, Ike, and Khrushchev.

Asian flu would hit us hard—
got me carried home from school
by Mr. Savarire, the principal.

Elsewhere seeds for a revolt were sown
by Betty Friedan at a Smith reunion.
I later worked with her at NOW.

At this height of the Beat era
San Francisco's City Lights
was raided by the POLICE for publishing

Allen Ginsberg's *Howl.* The National Guard
of Arkansas tried to stop
some little kids just our size

from integrating Little Rock.
We were still innocent. I sent
a thank-you note to Miss McGowan.

Moon Ride

We drive east to catch October
Leaves-Falling-Moon rising
over Escambia Bay in Pensacola
where autumn is not.

Blue birds, robins arrive to stay or dally
on their way to Mexico. New growth
appears on plants like the palmetto palms
I didn't know existed. The world is upside down.

But this autumn moon over the sea
anchors me, my natural rhythm
swaying more with moon than sun—
dreaming of moon-viewing parties.

At the Bay Bridge Dairy Queen
we stop, share this viewing space
with motorcycle riders. The water
sparkles like moon on prairie snow.

A Time for Herons

August. No one should work in this month of heat that wears heavy like a raccoon overcoat.

We laze about on our sailboat on the Chesapeake Bay. Read escape literature. Feed the hissing swans.

We decide to take a voyage south to Smith Island, an island that was settled in the 1600s by the English. Their descendants stayed, intermarried, and died here as the world moved ahead. Now the civilized escape to Smith Island for quiet, seafood, and an authentic Elizabethan accent.

After a meal of big blue crabs, corn fritters, and fried oysters, we return to our boat to watch the sunset. Then a racket overhead. We are docked next to a heron rookery. Nests like small haystacks flutter and shriek with great blue heron chicks. Heron already the size of pterodactyls want their dinner. Parents are busy bringing in bluefish carry-out. We watch until the sunset fades summer-red on the bay.

For years I dream of big birds on an island that resists time, with the sun rising on small white gravestones of people who knew only this hidden home.

sky
water
heron time

Stargazing at Noon

The planetarium trip with Dr. Cosmos
and The Star Hoppers is a carnival ride
on a spaceship with rappers. The sky ceiling
shines, but not as bright as winter sky
over South Dakota, where Orion,
the dog Sirius, and Diana hunt
and bark as close as the neighbor's farm.
Here stars born of clouds and dust
and gases crashing together might be sisters
or brothers to the cattle. The rings of Saturn
made of ice and snow and dust mirror
the Great Plains storms. Planets
conceived from leftover stars glow as the lover
Venus and rusty Mars look to be a short day trip
at most, via the Milky Way Express.
Shivering under a shooting star,
the stardust in my body reaches out
toward that playground where rides
are free and tickets dissolve in dark.

Wounded Knee Horseback Ride
   (December 28, 2000)

*A ceremony to commemorate the 110th massacre
at Wounded Knee in 1890*

The *Sioux Falls Argus Leader* chronicles
the Big Foot Memorial Ride from

Sitting Bull's camp across the frozen
South Dakota plains, through The Badlands, to Pine Ridge.

Blizzard blowing, horses moving stiffly,
sixty riders—mostly young—descended

from slaughtered Minniconjou, Hunkpapa Sioux,
warmed by camaraderie, campfires, soup.

Arctic wind cannot compete
with the stone-cold end of a mass grave.

Behind the concrete apron and chain-link fence
sits an empty church foundation sprayed with

old graffiti; a small arch of reddened brick,
cinder blocks and iron. Grass stretches away.

A single marble column names the victims:
Big Foot, his braves, many women and children.

A bag of Christmas candy and an apple
lie at the marble base; blue sky surrounds.

All is bigger, smaller, and more stark
in the prairie vastness.

Photos from the Denver Public Library
show the frozen dead in the snow—

twisted, dumped in a grave,
soldiers posing nearby given medals.

Indians held as prisoners
on their own land: tuberculosis,

cigarettes, diabetes, alcohol,
commodities dispersed.

Sun shines on the winter prairie.
The turtle's heart beats on in death.

II

Hiawatha Asylum

The Indian Wars never ended in this country.
—Joy Harjo, "Witness,"
The Woman Who Fell from the Sky

Finding Hiawatha

Highway 18 runs past the grain elevators
to Hiawatha Golf Club near
the local hospital. Club restrooms
read: "Braves" and "Squaws."
In the middle of the fairway
lies a graveyard—fenced—
between the fifth and seventh hole:
sunken remains of 120 men and women who died
at the Hiawatha Asylum for Insane Indians.

Travelers might note the ski hill to the west
of Route 18—once the site of winter Olympic trials.
The city bought the old Asylum grounds
with the stipulation it be used
for "recreational use." No mention
of sacred ground on these soft Coteau des Prairies.

A faded prayer flag flutters in the wind.
A sign near the small burial plot reads:
"Please do not play balls from the rough."
A monument lists the names of the dead:
Blue Sky, Long Time Owl Woman,
Yells at Night, Red Crow,
James Crow Lightning, Edith Standing Bear.
The golfers play through without a glance.

South Dakota Senator Richard Pettigrew's Senate Floor Plea, 1899*

An effort to obtain federal funds for an "Indian insane asylum" in South Dakota

It has been well established that the percentage
of insanity is greater among half-breeds
than among the full-blooded Indians.
This is explained by the theory
of cross-breeding, that has a tendency
to weaken the race.
For this reason it is confidently expected
by those who have made a study of these conditions
that the rate of insanity will greatly increase
as our civilization develops. The peculiar mental
afflictions of the Indians make it impractical
to treat them in connection with whites.
Association with their ancient enemy has,
it is said, a harrowing effect upon them.
Also, it has been demonstrated by experience
that the various state asylums for the treatment
of the insane are not kindly disposed
toward receiving Indian patients.

found poem

How to Get Committed to the Hiawatha Asylum for Insane Indians

First, you must be Chippewa, Navajo,
Pawnee, Lakota, Crow, or Winnebago.

Dance the Ghost Dance
to bring back the buffalo.

Have a seizure and fall down—
but the easiest way: anger an Indian agent.

Get in a loud argument with your wife's
brother because he said she sounded like a crow.

Talk to your dead ancestors about
what troubles you. Pray for their wisdom.

Believe you are White Buffalo Woman—
hold pipe ceremonies for days with no sleep.

Carry a congenital deformity
or become senile.

Tell your teacher you don't care
about Pilgrims and want to study Crazy Horse.

Refuse to let your children go
to the Carlisle Boarding School.

Conduct a healing ceremony
with special herbs for your mother.

Have a party with a group of cousins
and friends. Get rowdy, wake the Indian agent.

Reject Christianity,
refuse Western medicine.

Live on an Indian reservation
in the middle of nowhere.

Get drunk and lie down in fire.

Augustana Academy Student Writes Her Family (September 8, 1929)

I like the school, but I miss you so much.
Last week we went out to the Indian Insane Asylum
for a picnic. We shared lunches with the patients.
It made me sad. They seem so sad—
like Grandpa was when Grandma died.
One older woman cried the whole time. I think
her name is Blue Sky. I like the Indian names because
they sound like poems. They paint pictures reminding
me of birds and landscapes. Blue Sky's
long black hair, like cousin Mary's, looks like
a wave of first-plowed dirt at sunrise. She wants
to go home to her people. I understand.
Even a reservation must be better than some
brick building on the hill. I bet she'd rather
have food she can cook herself and eat with family.
I'm not sure how their food tastes. Our food
is pretty good. Last night we had corn on the cob
and rhubarb pie for dessert. I know you are busy
with the harvest now. There is a grain elevator
across the street, and the pink corn dust settles
all over town like a winter sunset.

Dr. Silk Writes Home (March 20, 1929)

Dr. Samuel Silk, a psychiatrist from St. Elizabeth's Hospital in Washington, DC, was dispatched to investigate problems at the Hiawatha Asylum for Insane Indians in Canton, South Dakota.

The trip was long, the Appalachians
giving way to a vast unknown
of land where towns spring full blown from fields.
March is winter here: few signs
of spring. No cherry blossoms. In this place
the wind wails constantly, competes
with angry gods of mud and melting snow.
The Chinese *Canton* strikes one odd
where so many speak Norwegian,
celebrating Scandinavian feasts.
The grasses once were taller than these Nords.
This sea of green swallowed up some whole.
Ghosts of a buried prairie shimmer,
haunting the flat horizon.

Long Time Owl Woman Haunts the Canton Hospital

Last night I heard a clumsy bird
whirl in like a sick
stumbling buffalo. It coughed
and landed on the spit of cement.
A bad omen, this bird that swallows
the sick into its swollen belly,
flies straight up and leaves.
My people healed with help
from the natural world. Not machines
and surgery. I've seen strange things
while wandering the hospital halls: hurt
babies in plastic boxes crying and no one there.
I want to comfort them, but can't.
I couldn't comfort those little ones born
at the Asylum. I sang for them, but then
they were gone like the owl in the morning.
The night is my home. Sometimes now
I whistle to the dying.

Dr. Silk Writes Home (March 21, 1929)

The problems are enormous already.
My days are long. We went between
two buildings of the hospital—the wind
blew snow straight in my face. Your long wool scarf
was welcome. Thank you. Conditions
are dubious. Patient with a tumor
on the brain was locked in solitude
so others could not see him. Another
secluded in a room to prevent fights.
Not necessary, I shall request his release.
A straitjacketed boy on the cold floor,
retarded, chamber pot uncovered, full.
Another epileptic shut away. A place
of padlocks and chamber pots. There are so many.
I feel as though I've fallen into a darker decade.

Yells At Night

Nurse's note

Last night his cries pierced my dreams.
I checked, but could not penetrate the pain.
Who bestowed this name
without a melody or meaning, blaming him?
Many patients lose their given names
to ignorance of native tongues. Many,
committed for refusing to speak
our own words. The sounds last night
bore an ancient rhythm beating from the earth.
Perhaps he once performed the Ghost Dance
and dreams of buffalo and antelope
that return, the men who corralled him
disappearing like some summer storm
blowing winds of disaster, then leaving prairie sun.

Dr. Silk Writes Home (March 22, 1929)

During my breakfast at the hotel
(which was pretty good with fresh eggs
and corn-fed bacon, crisp as October)
I noticed a cabinet with "souvenirs"
from the asylum for sale. A customer
exclaimed over the fine detail on a painted plate
from a "crazy Indian." I bristled as the clerk
laughed and rang up the sale. The city touts
the asylum as an attraction, "a spectacular treat
to complete a shopping day in Canton."
Patients string beads into necklaces, handbags,
and weave baskets of strong prairie grasses. Blue Sky
handed me one the other day, smiled. A gift that
would be rude to refuse. You will enjoy it.
Quill chokers quiver with colors of this lonely
landscape. I see therapeutic value in creative activity,
but the patients do not reap the profits. The citizens
are pleased to have a federal facility that brings
good income to town. But I don't think
it will be here much longer. Findings
are not auspicious for continuation.
The patients do not receive half
the attention you give your African violets.

Augustana Academy Student Writes Family
(October 4, 1929)

Last night I heard five rings
on our dorm phone, signal
of an Asylum Indian escape.
I was studying late for a test
when it shrilled through
like a coyote's call. I'd run, too.
When we last visited the place
to sing hymns for the patients
I saw a girl who made me cry—
her hair matted. Dirty flowered dress
made for a woman, not a girl.
Only about ten, I think.
She didn't talk; her eyes beamed fear.
Can kids be crazy? How would I know
if I were crazy? I'd flee like deer
to the woods if I were her. Farm wives
would hide her in their barns, feed her.
No one is afraid of the Indians.

Dr. Silk Writes Home (March 23, 1929)

I talked with the laundress today.
I don't blame her for the filthy bedclothes
on the wards: black as dirt. She is kept busy
with curtains and notes: *We have a good many,
and they are hard to iron. The patients lie
on bedspreads with shoes on,* she laments;
the wash is not as white as I'd like.
The heat is coal, the water hard.
She wants a permanent ironing board,
electric iron. I spoke with her of allegations
that Miss Fillious antagonizes the staff.
She reported *no difficulties of any kind with her.*
The problem here is not the head nurse.
Or laundry. Deeper than dirt;
lye soap will not wash it away.

Hiawatha Volunteer

It makes me sad to visit
the Indians at the Insane Asylum.
Last week I gave Long Time Owl Woman
a bath and she just cried. She's getting frail.
Wants to go home to her people.
I can't blame her. I'd miss my family.
That Dr. H is not so nice. Why send
someone like him? He can't even drive
a tractor. I don't know what he does.
Never seen him in town. He's always
"having a bit to eat" at that nice home
they built for him. Lives alone.
No family. No wife. No kids.
Who'd live with him? The Indians
don't like him. There is nothing wrong
with them. Why Aunt Alma
has the same falling-down fits
and her sister Ruth looks after her.
It's nothing bad. Just happens.
Like TB. People have broken parts.
You just live with it. Help out. No need
to throw them out or lock them away.
We've all got a few rusted, busted pieces.
We just patch them up the best we can
and go on. Bake a pie.

Dr. Silk Writes Home (March 24, 1929)

This has been a trying day
and I would welcome
your wise womanly counsel.
Dr. Hummer has a solid
streak of misogyny running
down the back of his white coat.
He dislikes nurses. I had no desire
to enter this fracas, as I considered it
an internal matter. However,
during my interviews with staff I was
drawn into their quarrel.
There's raged a furious feud
between head nurse and Hummer
since she arrived. Miss F, a thirtyish woman
with a penchant for turquoise scarves,
exhibits neatness and professionalism.
Well qualified, with good training,
she is energetic and shows a sympathetic attitude
toward patients. I believe you would
get on well with her. She enjoys
reading poetry, especially Gerard Manley Hopkins.
Dr. H. insists the kitchen and dining-room staff,
along with laborers, furnish affidavits on her.
I suspect they may have thought this necessary
in order to keep their jobs. You will appreciate
one complaint by a young, dining-room girl
that Miss F *carried on* at the dinner table
telling stories and *associated with women
in town who drank.* The girl did not think
such was *ladylike,* nor was a previous
employee who *smoked cigarettes.* She huffed
that she *was not brought up that way!*

But this is a diversion, my dear. There is great
sadness residing here under the cottonwoods.
These cold, clear nights I miss you most.

Dr. Hummer Defends Himself

From 1908 to its closing in 1933, Dr. Hummer served as superintendent of the Hiawatha Asylum.

I did not choose this place.
Dr. White recommended me.
When young, I thought it would be
an adventure to go West. But it was
a mistake, this godforsaken field
of wild Indians—forty-three different tribes.
I can't get any histories; their tongue
is gibberish to me. Sure, many of the patients
are asymptomatic. But they can't go home
since they are "below normal," and must be
sterilized first. I have no means to do this.
The Asylum doesn't meet
standards, but what can I do?
I was not trained to treat Indians.

Night Train

I recall when the Asylum closed. I was a girl.
We lived just east of Hiawatha then.
Perhaps it was November when the cold
hunkers down to stay. Outside, that night,
geese honking through clouds, I heard
the train whistle for the patients, their long ride
beckoning to St. Elizabeth's in Washington, DC.
They huddled in blankets, waited by big iron gates,
the wind hurling around them. Empty building
hulked behind, that long dark winter solstice
shadowing all. Still, I thought, the city
may frighten them more. Here on the prairie
there's a certain quiet of sky and space.

Death at Hiawatha

The Lincoln County Courthouse recorded
one-hundred eighty-nine Asylum deaths,

an inauspicious start
for seven children born there.

Average age at death was forty-two;
most common cause: tuberculosis.

Typical non-Indian death: an octogenarian
Norwegian farmer killed by lightning while plowing.

The best way to catch TB:
crowd people into poorly ventilated space
like German death camps.

Patients were not screened. Sputum exams
or chest x-rays could have saved many.

In South Dakota's surplus space, fresh air
they could not breathe.

Dr. Silk Writes Home (March 25, 1929)

Today I had them apply restraints to me.
Only briefly attached with wristlets,
but patients endure entire nights like this.
I saw iron rings in Baltimore
at City Hospital where they chained
patients to walls. In Canton, the restraints
are kept by the financial clerk.
A *ward attendant* with no medical credentials
decides if a patient is to be restrained
and *the clerk* hands him the apparatus.
The practice stems from old wars and fears,
not illness. These patients are not criminals.
I am ready to be released and return home.

Canton Farmer Remembers

My dad and I worked at the old Asylum.
Piggery, dairy, corn cribs, horse barn, fields.
Just one farmer up there, no hands.
We did thrashing with Crazy Charlie—epileptic.
Hog butchered. Wasn't a very sanitary operation;
drainage bad. The women sat outside
in summer. Smiled and waved. Seemed real nice.
Big business in this corn and soybean county.
The town didn't want to lose that Fed money.
They shut down when we needed them the most—
Depression years. We don't talk of that place.
Kind of shameful. When they golf, they play around
that little cemetery with no markers.

Long Time Owl Woman Haunts Hiawatha Golf Course

I watch the locals
chase their balls in carts
around my burial ground.
I want to laugh,
lament: Hiawatha
Indian Insane
Asylum. Which we were not.
I was sent here to die away
from my people because
the Indian agent said
my fits and visions were crazy.
My grandmother had them, too.
They help us see the unseen.
They are good. Not bad.
Fenced in death, in life
we could not be controlled.
My curse upon their scores!
Twisted be their swings!
Their balls, Gone! Laughing
I soar above the pines,
over these unmarked graves,
the broken doctors, bodies
left here by the fleeting
trickster on his path.

III

Branching Out: Looking for Home

The journey is my home.
—Muriel Rukeyser, *One Life*

The Inner Circle

I had not thought death had undone so many
—Dante Alighieri, Inferno

The aerial photograph depicts
the sandstone sanatorium
as a circle with eight spokes.

Inside lies a courtyard. Rehabilitation.
Purgatory. Residential Treatment.
Protected from wrathful winds,

the green lawn writhes smoke.
This island on a red-dirt hill
centers a Plains dark wood

where bodies and spirits
linger, languish, speak of demon wars.
Exiled, banished here among

red Folgers coffee-can ashtrays
scattered like gravestones among
the picnic tables and portable BBQs.

Vague shapes gesticulate
in heated smoke huts during Dakota winters
through the semi-opaque glass.

Vestiges of long ago—days of free-issue
cigarettes and twenty-five-cent beer—
remembered in the Circle of Death.

One-time executives, professors, businessmen
with drifters, grifters, convicts of the same
lamentation, loss, regret.

All fallen from different heights
into booze, drugs, crack, hooch
sliding down addiction's slope.

Bodies tattooed with indulgences
ache with hepatitis C and HIV,
missing teeth, hearing, sensation.

Small groups segregate in rain and snow—
breaking into smaller circles
Indians, cowboys, women,

African-American, PTSD, young, old.
Loners watch like sentinels.
Mallards fly in, petunias and peonies bloom in smoke.

A powwow dancer drums the earth—forgotten
half-remembered dreams of peace.
An Easter-egg hunt races by. Seasons

come and go like vets. Truth and lies mingle
with the smoke, float
into hard blue prairie sky. Clouds

hoping for a contrail to ride out of here
beyond Lost River mist traversed
on the way into the inner circle.

Smoking Mr. V

The best part of his day was smoking.
Quadriplegic, blind—his home a VA
hospital bed—he needed a hand.
So twice a shift I held his cigarette,

into his lips, then out—a rhythm
easy enough for a Red Cross volunteer
who smoked him after school,
Tuesdays, Thursdays, 1962.

Since WWII, my dad smoked too.
Mr. V, who fought in WWI,
was older than my grandfather, and yet
he always greeted me, *Hi, Beautiful*

Gray shrunken shadow of a man,
his body concentrated at the core—
a giant head and heart worked overtime.
He listened to his bedside radio.

So, did you hear Paul Harvey?
Always something new to chat about
during the smoke. He had few visitors.
Not everybody called me beautiful.

Evening Shift

A different time—like story time—
the patient quiet. Eyes closed, sighs.
I rub on medication-scented Dermassage
and for twenty minutes rub
the hospital away like chalk
from a blackboard full of care.

Lulled, relaxed, her muscles slack—
she talks about the accident.
Sometimes she cries, from the marrow,
the body speaking its own story.

Hotel Hot Springs

They come from Denver, Kalispell,
Cheyenne, Grand Junction—all over the West—
to this small Black Hills town. Lakota winter
camping grounds—the Minnekahta—
veterans with nowhere else to go.
TB. Shell shock. No job, no wife, no home.
The river that never freezes claims mornings lost
in January and February mist.

A safe place to survive the blizzards howling
destitute, out of control, shelter sought,
the prairie frozen. Well-to-do and ill
arrived by rail to seek the healing waters
years ago; resorts run down become
the dark dives that line the riverbanks.

Veterans of World War I and II
checked into this old sanatorium
turned VA clinic—domiciliary
to stay for years forever. Domed red roof,
the wings hexagonal jut out toward town.

Later come more wars: Vietnam,
Persian Gulf. Afghanistan. Iraq.
The wounded drifting and spilling
into cheap hotels—the Buffalo,
Frontier, and Waterside last resorts
for bikers cowboys broken-down broken-up
men no one to love nowhere to go.

Winding into town between soft red
clay hills, the billboard shouts a welcome:
"Hot Springs—The Veteran's Town."

Rock Man

A large tree trunk of a man,
oak or maybe river cottonwood—
if trees wore camouflage suspenders.

He prefers badgers to men.
Not a group on communication skills,
after years of booze and blackouts

this seems foreign to him. Unnecessary.
His ideal: a cabin so deep in the woods
only wolves penetrate.

Land fenced high,
his solitude secured with barbed wire.
Only animals, vegetables, minerals allowed.

I engage with questions of his world.
Recognize rocks and seashells
as Jungian symbols of the Self.

But self-educated by land, sea and sky
he teaches me the fossils of the Plains—
ferns and shellfish preserved

in rocks, unnoticed. He speaks their lives.
Later he brings me a trilobite—small,
smooth as Buddha's tummy for rubbing.

Maybe he is a buddha, understanding
the nonverbal: *no birth, no death,*
the unspoken knowledge of rocks.

Anomie

My sociology student defined
anomie as "a small brown bear."

I decree *anomie* Florida,
"the state with the prettiest name."

Developments and palms
the thriving, dominant weeds.

The place I live, Millstone,
fielded Navy helicopters years ago.

Hummers hulk in driveways
but no clotheslines are allowed.

A walking path stands empty
until a parrot on a leash strolls by.

Streets stunt into cul-de-sacs
leading to Hotel California.

Swimming pools lounge
in cages, atrophy with neon toys.

Balloon sculptures of black cats, snowmen
loom on lawns, shift seasonally in the wind—

scare the teacup poodles sporting painted nails,
rhinestone sweaters, disposable dispositions.

Escambia County Ambulance
steals in for a new body weekly.

Golf carts buzz down walks
on Sunday afternoons knocking

Mormon missionaries
into Monday.

A skateboard slams by, child
wide-eyed, fleeing for his life.

Surplus Beans

Like those Poor Laws of England
there is an Overseer of the Poor
in Jackson County. He decides
who deserves chicken or cheese.

Color and family reputation figure in.
Butter rare as bricks of gold. The chickens
turn green in cans, but beans endure.
Extension department agents

with their mimeographed recipes
and strained smiles swarm back roads
determined to teach the poor 114 ways
to love the bean: lima, pinto, navy.

The struggle grinds Stella down
to dust too fine for making bread.

Bookstore Church

The faithful form a ragged line
early on Sunday mornings
outside Barnes & Noble. The throng
swells with earnest supplicants
seeking books, truth, God
and they alone could say what.
Maybe it's only Starbucks coffee.
A slouched young man
reads a Batman comic, muttering.
In over-padded chairs
a mother and daughters observe
postmodern reading rituals.
A family of four
fingers pages like rosary beads while
eating croissants over magazines.
A woman in green leotards is entrenched
near a window with Martha Stewart.
Students surrounded with reference books
work through Purgatory toward
a term paper due Monday.
A couple in the back peruses new
poetry selections, reading some aloud.
A brother and sister sprawl on the floor
in the children's section during a rare
communion between sibling spats.
A blonde reverently sips her cappuccino,
table spread with the *New York Times*
Music choirs from new CDs.
All browse contentedly—
no creed to recite or sermon
to endure. Good coffee. Benediction.

Goodwill

During the week
of Thanksgiving
a cabless semitruck
open, unattended
sulks in the city parking lot
waiting to be filled.
Wind bays in drain spouts
ice congeals.
I drop off four
boxes of books
a text
on poverty in America
lands on top.
By Friday the truck,
is three-quarters full—
clear-blue plastic bags
contain worn tennis shoes
ragged striped towels
all sizes of closet discards
toys played out.
One beige appliance
in parts I can't identify.
I've heard that people sometimes
leave sheets soiled with semen
at homeless shelters.
The season of giving
now underway as Christmas
lights go up and the Salvation
Army sends its soldiers
into battle armed with bells.

Hannah's House:
A Shelter for Women and Children

1. Security Room

Quarters cramped as a ship's with small squares
of white floor not much bigger
than a checkerboard. Metal bunk beds line
the plain room with mix-matched
floral/striped sheets, blankets, and bedspreads.
Under the beds black bags
bulge with clothes, belongings.
Off the beds hang rainbow-colored layers
of clothes for job interviews and court appearances.
A tiny window without a curtain admits a dab of sun
too embarrassed to look closely. A chair
is a nightstand for glasses, keys,
a favorite toy, a pacifier to comfort nightmares.
No privacy. As many as fifteen a week.
The room tests new residents.
Can they get along with others? Do they steal or fight?
In a space so tight most couldn't tolerate—
babies cry sick, workers return late
or leave before dawn for their jobs—always
with kids in tow. No time to make beds or make neat.
Boys and girls curl into pretzels, bounce
their heads against top bunk beds. One woman sings
Row, row, row your boat, and a boy, not her own,
chimes in from the trundle bed.

2. Rita's Journal

I never wrote good in school.
Too many rules. But I wrote a poem once
about my dog, Junior. Dad used to give him
a bowl of beer on Friday nights then laugh
his crazy ass off while Junior stumbled
around trying to kiss the cat. It was funny,
but the teacher didn't laugh. I never kept no
journal before, but the social worker gave us these—
said we could write anything—not worry
about spelling or rules. She read some poems
from a woman that sounded like me. Love troubles.
Me, I thought he was a good egg. Met him
at church. Then he started drinkin' and druggin'
so I did too. We slid down real fast into a big,
fat mud puddle. Split up. I like knowing
I'm not alone. We all got troubles.

3. Gina and Willie

Dancing to Willie Nelson on her pink radio
with the coat-hanger antenna,
she closes her eyes and enters a world
of home with flying squirrels, black bears

while cooing: *fussy little white boy, you hold
your head up real good.* Her children
can't live with her until she *gets
her shit together.*

For this song she is as loving tender
as any mom managing carpools.
Her broken knuckles soft.
She's not in a fighting mood today.

4. Dorothea's Diary

It was scary to go to the shelter
the day I made that decision. I sat at JB's Truck Stop
drinking coffee—thinking.

Do I keep hitching rides to nowhere?
I was tired. I felt like a trucker
at the end of a run from Frisco to Philly.

The shelter looked like any house in any
seedy neighborhood. Patsy Cline lived
down the street once—or so I heard. I was "crazy" like she sang.

The prison-gray steel door had a note:
Knock Loudly. I did—holding my breath.
Inside I heard someone shout, *Keep it down!*

We're a shelter, not a circus. A kid flew by
as I went down the short hall to the office.
Signs read: *No smoking on front porch.*

Curfew for women with children: 8:00 p.m.
I signed a paper saying it was true—
I had no home

or resources for one.
I would abide by the rules.
I'm still here. Biding

my time. Abiding by the rules.

5. Jump Starts

At picnics Dad got drunk
stood us in water, shot at our feet
then sat us down to hot dogs—
Your last meal—enjoy it. Those hot dogs
tasted better than
red-velvet birthday cake, but
I don't eat them anymore. I got good
jumping high and fast. Comes in handy since
my husband hits, drinks, yells a lot.
No guns—just sick and mean. Won't let me
see my sisters or square dance.
Don't want our kids drinking any
of his goddamn beer.
I finally told him, *Look, I survived
breast cancer, a heart attack,
years of abuse. I'm going to live.
Maybe even take a cruise.* I did.
Came back to rub his back,
fetch his cigarettes, pills, and booze.
We've had some love, some fun.
The cancer's fucking back.
I'm tired now—
can't jump no more.
After all those practice deaths
this last one should be easy.
Shit, when that last gun goes off
I'll be way out front of the crowd
headed for heaven or hell.

6. Letty Writes Her Sister

The light here is dim, the table wobbly.
I don't belong. This place is hell—
harassed, sad women, kids with bags
beneath their eyes. I cry a lot, don't sleep,
but at least the kids are still with me.
Thanks for putting our things in storage
again. I go every day to get what we need.
The kids wanted crayons. I got mom's quilt—
the one she made from pieces of old flannel
pajamas and that tacky taffeta formal.
But it's a comfort to me. Then I go to the library
for more books. I'm reading *Montana Sky*
by Nora Roberts. Her women are stronger
than me. They rope and ride like you.
Sam's asthma's bad, but Janie's healthy
this year. They draw pictures and write stories
for me and you. All of the kids have friends.
Most of them are well behaved. Some pray
before every meal without being told.
I'm thankful, but I want my own house back.
I hope you get off your GM shift on time.
We could go out someplace nice. Like Applebee's.
The food here's mostly canned.
I want a salad, some spices.

7. Shelter Kitchen

No windowsill
geraniums

or pot of Earl Grey tea
on an oak table.

No dog or cat food bowls
on the floor.

Fred's Feed & Seed wall calendar
minus piano lessons, birthday parties.

A huge refrigerator (no drawings)
holds five gallons of sweet pickles;

the freezer bulges with eight turkeys
leftover mashed potatoes—Thanksgiving

every week. Steel pots on the stove
small buddhas in dim light.

8. Tonia

My mama called me her "love child."
Now I got four "love childs." I love
their Daddy, too. James just not mature. He bought
an old Harley. We got out of the city
so the kids don't have to barricade themselves
inside to keep away from the guns, drug dealers,
when I'm at work. I was working pretty hard
at the bathtub factory days, cleaning the hospital nights.
Then I broke my ankle. Got welfare for a while—
$350 a month, but the rent was $351. I had to sell
a few food stamps to get that extra dollar.
James couldn't get a job so we came to the shelter.

When my ankle heals I'm going back
to work. Problem is I need a car—
James wrecked mine. Then he left.
I want a home with all my kids together.
Keep up their grades, chores, church. Last week
the shelter went to Washington. We saw statues,
the White House, all kinds of folk from overseas.
The kids got so excited. I want my kids
to see things, go places. Remember to be kind.
Like yesterday, at the bus stop a little girl
was shivering so I gave her my hooded sweatshirt.
My kids asked, *How come you did that mama?*
I said, *Because we all somebody's love child.*

9. Tara Writes to Hannah's House

I'm living in Tennessee and pickin'
up that accent. Drawlin' like Dolly.
I remember it from when I was a kid.
I'm back with my dad. He's still an asshole,
but said I could stay a few weeks. His wife,
the one with plastic tits, is pissed,
but he owes me. I found out my old best friend
Susie got shot by her bad-news boyfriend.
After the shelter I did OK but lost my job
at Burger King. Went back to drinking beer.
Jack Daniels when someone bought it.
But I needed a place to stay, so came here.
So what's up at the shelter? Did Gina find a job?
Did Cammy get her kids back? I think about you guys
all the time. You were the best family this chick
ever had. Just wanted you to know I'm still alive.
I'm back working on my GED. Met a new dude
in night school. He's cool as chrome.

Seeing Myself

At the mall I see another woman
wearing the candy-cane sweater
I donated to Hannah's House.

Here is a woman, also small,
smiling at me, a stranger.
An odd feeling—
like seeing myself
walk into a mirror,
abracadabra-ed into

a different race, limping,
herding three kids.
Approaching from the other side
of some invisible line
that any woman
might be pushed across.

Blackberry Winter: A Southern Term

After the blackberry vines have blossomed
as tiny rose clusters and somewhere around
Easter-basket time or when dogwoods bark,

the Siberian Express dips south with a load
of cold. It laughs as the parkas and mittens
come out and gardens are covered with sheets

in Alabama and Georgia. It's a brief visit
like Indian Summer—but this an unwelcome blast—
everyone wants to leave immediately.

A lovely term—deeply rich plum smelling
like grandma's jelly in Ball jars glowing
in the sun. If only it would visit in July.

A Few Wars Ago: Levertov's "At the
Justice Department November 15, 1969"

I was there breathing
the same *brown gas-fog*
as a poet I did not yet know
but would later admire.
We both wanted the war
in Asia to end and stumbled
hand in hand with half a million
others protesting and gasping
into a night wet-cold like fever and chills.

Earlier we marched past
the White House and shouted
the name of a dead warrior
while the FBI popped photos.
I was a VISTA volunteer,
AWOL from my post in Indiana.
But this was where I needed
to be that November day—
beneath the street lamps
of the Justice Department
with Denise Levertov
gasping for breath and peace.

* *VISTA (Volunteers in Service to America) was a federal program founded in 1965 and is now called AmeriCorps VISTA.*

Snapshots in Haiku

Dakota bar—
the bride wears white
cowboy boots

winter night
a black-and-white fox walks
through my dream

April rain—
their newly planted maple
strung with Christmas lights

Saturday morning
local café steams
coffee and politics

after the storm
a basketball hoop
filled with snow

November
wings of heron disappear
into dusk

summer afternoon . . .
flute music wafts in window
with a fly

three turtles sunning
pause at the pond's edge—
man on a backhoe

summer matinee
the hot-flash musical
Menopause

Sunday morning—
downtown streets belong
to the homeless

Christmas season
toilet seat at Flea Market
mended with red tape

Upper Peninsula of Michigan

The locals taught me where to find morels—
those mysteries of dark earth places
that delight if you surprise them
hiding like kids in a mountain
of leaves—if you don't choose the poisonous
cousins by mistake. They showed me
how to dance dandelions and grapes
into wines; how to snowshoe out the second-
story window and laugh about it.
What could I teach them?

Feral Peacocks

One day the peacocks just arrived:
escaped, no doubt, from a nearby farm.
They roosted in the tall sycamores
beside the creek among the sheep
and close to the birdfeeder.
Basic needs all met, free of human schedules,
they entertain us. Male displays
with rattling feathers dance, amused us
through several reruns. But even
casual strutting (blue-green tails folded,
all eyes closed) enchanted us—
especially during winter. Wild and tame
they settled in, even when icicles hung
like frozen beards. No snow birds, these tough dudes.
They cry that shrill that human cry: "Help! Help!"
on eerie nights. It left us wondering.
Flannery O'Connor kept them as pets
on her Georgia farm among her feral souls.

Benita's Photo

At Fourteenth and Constitution
between the FBI and Smithsonian—
in February slush and valentines

the photography professor focuses
her 35-millimeter black-and-white eye.
The woman subject sleeps, snores

on a grate with steam
shrouding her stillness.
Cars and walkers, urban glazed

by policy and lawmaking pass
her beauty. Hands of a Michelangelo
gnarled in prayer, captured in light.

Her photo hangs next to our front door.
Here people pause on leaving,
beckoned by the hands.

Homeless at McDonald's

A mother and grown daughter live quietly
in a blue Chevy van parked at McDonald's
at Forty-First and Minnesota.
Rusted van, a window duct-taped shut,
packed to the roof with boxes, blankets, lamps.
The mother limps on bandaged foot, balances
coffee, her daughter shuffling behind
with Egg McMuffins and condiments.
Here they eat and use the restroom
near the brightly colored kiddies' playground.
Homeless women aren't in ads or jingles.
Management doesn't police the parking lot.
The staff can picture being in that car—
knows everyone can't live in comfortable
homes too busy to cook healthy meals
with soccer, dance, piano, basketball.
McDonald's meals are happy ones with toys.
These women live here, hiding furtively—
a movement in the dumpster's neon shadow—
homeless incorporate beneath
the golden arches of America.

Author's Note

The poems in Part II of this book, Hiawatha Asylum, are based on research into the Canton Asylum for Insane Indians that my late husband, Brad Soule, and I did in the early 2000s, when we first moved to Canton, South Dakota. As mental-health professionals, we were surprised that we had never heard of this place. I grew up in Sioux Falls, yet I never heard a whisper about its existence. Several of my poems are based on letters written in 1929 by Samuel Silk, MD, a psychiatrist from St. Elizabeth's mental hospital in Washington, DC, who was sent to investigate problems at the asylum. I used my imagination to write in various personas and voices, based on what I read in Silk's report. As I am not an Indigenous woman, I do not want to usurp any Native experience; instead, I focused on the facts and horror of the place. Brad and I did some of the first research on the asylum and conducted interviews with Canton residents who remembered it. I wanted to convey in poetry what happened at the asylum, and I believe poetry gives us a more human experience and creates space for empathy.

The poems in the first and third sections of the book address my love for the landscape of South Dakota and my concerns with social issues, such as the poverty I witnessed during my career as a social worker, educator, and clinician. These social issues are a focal point for me as a poet.

About the Author

Jennifer Soule has been a community organizer, scholar, and clinical worker. She is *professor emerita* in social work at Shepherd University in Shepherdstown, West Virginia. A South Dakota native with pioneer roots, she graduated from the University of South Dakota. She now lives in her hometown of Sioux Falls, a winter wonderland, with her dog Eliot. Her passion for place and language are well nurtured in South Dakota.

Soule's poems have appeared in several journals, including *South Dakota Review, Modern Haiku, The Sow's Ear Poetry Review,* and various anthologies. She's published two books: *Hiawatha Asylum* (Finishing Line Press, 2015) and *Postcard Days* (Cherry Grove Collections, 2019). With her late husband, Brad Soule, she edited an anthology, *Without Fear of Infamy,* which features the works of poets with ties to South Dakota (Scurfpea Press, 2019).

Soule received her MFA in creative writing from the University of Nebraska at age sixty-one—a degree that she pursued out of her passion for poetry. The MFA followed a successful career teaching social work—also a passion. Thus, she's an older, whole-grain woman from a land often dismissed—South Dakota—and she truly likes winter. Snow enthralls her. She loves the land, sky, people, and animals who have graced her long, eclectic life. All her roles—including being a caregiver for her hundred-year-old mom—enhance a sense of community with an appreciation of poetry as a touchpoint. She considers herself a well-seasoned woman deeply rooted in a nurturing locale, yet she's also eager to venture out to appreciate the whole range of humanity in its dignity and rich diversity.

www.ingramcontent.com/pod-product-compliance
Lightning Source LLC
Chambersburg PA
CBHW060915190426
43197CB00012BA/2498